Snow

Look for the other books on weather by

Marion Dane Bauer
Rain • Wind • Clouds
Rainbow • Sun

Simon Spotlight
An imprint of Simon & Schuster Children's Publishing Division
1230 Avenue of the Americas, New York, NY 10020
This Simon Spotlight edition May 2016
First Simon Spotlight edition August 2011
First Aladdin edition November 2003
Text copyright © 2003 by Marion Dane Bauer
Illustrations copyright © 2003 by John Wallace
For information about special discounts for bulk purchases, please contact
Simon & Schuster Special Sales at 1-866-506-1949
or business@simonandschuster.com.
Book design by Debra Sfetsios
The text of this book was set in Century Schoolbook.
Manufactured in the United States of America 0519 LAK
20 19
Library of Congress Cataloging-in-Publication Data
Bauer, Marion Dane.
Snow / Marion Dane Bauer ; illustrated by John Wallace.— 1st Aladdin
Paperbacks ed.
p. cm.
Summary: Simple text and illustration explore the wonders of snow.
1. Snow—Juvenile literature. [1. Snow.]
I. Wallace, John, 1966– ill. II. Title. III. Series.
QC924.7 .B38 2003
551.57'7—dc21
2002009524
ISBN 978-1-4814-6216-7 (hc)
ISBN 978-0-689-85437-8 (pbk)
ISBN 978-1-4424-9949-2 (eBook)

Snow

written by Marion Dane Bauer

illustrated by John Wallace

Ready-to-Read

Simon Spotlight
New York London Toronto Sydney New Delhi

The winter world is cold.

The trees are bare.

The grass is brown.

Gray clouds crawl
across the sky.

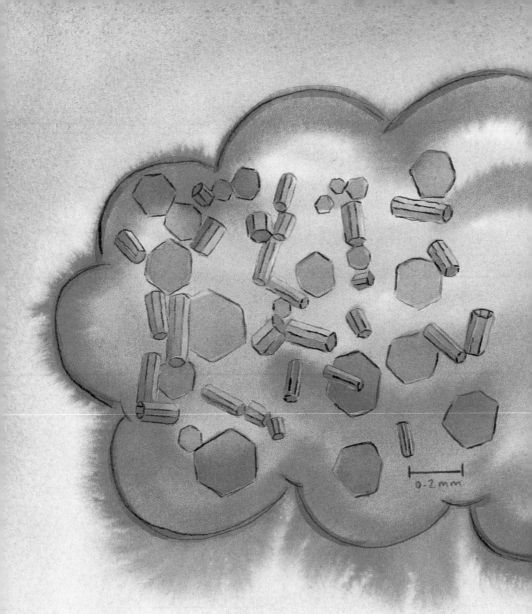

0.2 mm

Clouds are crystals of ice.

Each bit of ice
clings to a speck of dust.

The specks of ice and dust
cling to
one another.

They grow so heavy
that they drop
from the cloud.

Snow!

When the air is very cold,
the snowflakes stay small
and bright.

When the air is not so cold,
the flakes grow soft
and larger and larger.

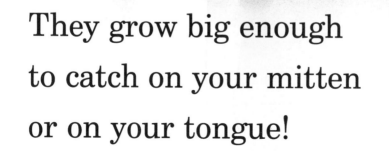

They grow big enough
to catch on your mitten
or on your tongue!

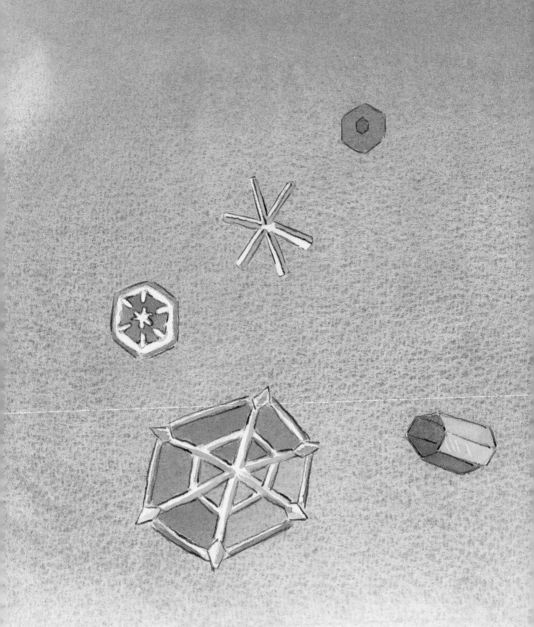

Each snowflake has six sides.

They come twirling
to the earth in a billion
different shapes.

Snow dresses the trees.

Snow covers the grass.

Snow keeps the flowers warm
through the long winter.

When spring comes,
snow melts into puddles,

into rivers,

into lakes,

and gives the earth
a fresh, cool drink.

But while winter is here,
snow makes the cold world
beautiful . . .

and so much fun!

Facts about snow:

* The temperature has to be thirty-two degrees or colder for water to turn into ice.

* Every snowflake has six sides.

* Every snowflake can contain as many as fifty crystals of ice.

* Trillions and trillions of snowflakes fall in a single storm, but the flakes take many different forms. People used to think it was impossible to find two alike, but a researcher named Nancy Knight once did find two snowflakes exactly alike.

* When strong winds drive heavy snow, we have a blizzard.

* Clouds can make snow even in summer, but because the summer air close to the earth is warm, the snow turns into rain by the time it reaches us.

ALSO BY

Marion Dane Bauer

Though you can't see the wind, you can
certainly feel it when the wind blows!
But where does wind come from?
The answer is at your fingertips.
Read about the wonders of wind. . . .

READY-TO-READ LEVEL 1

Wind

written by Marion Dane Bauer
Illustrated by John Wallace